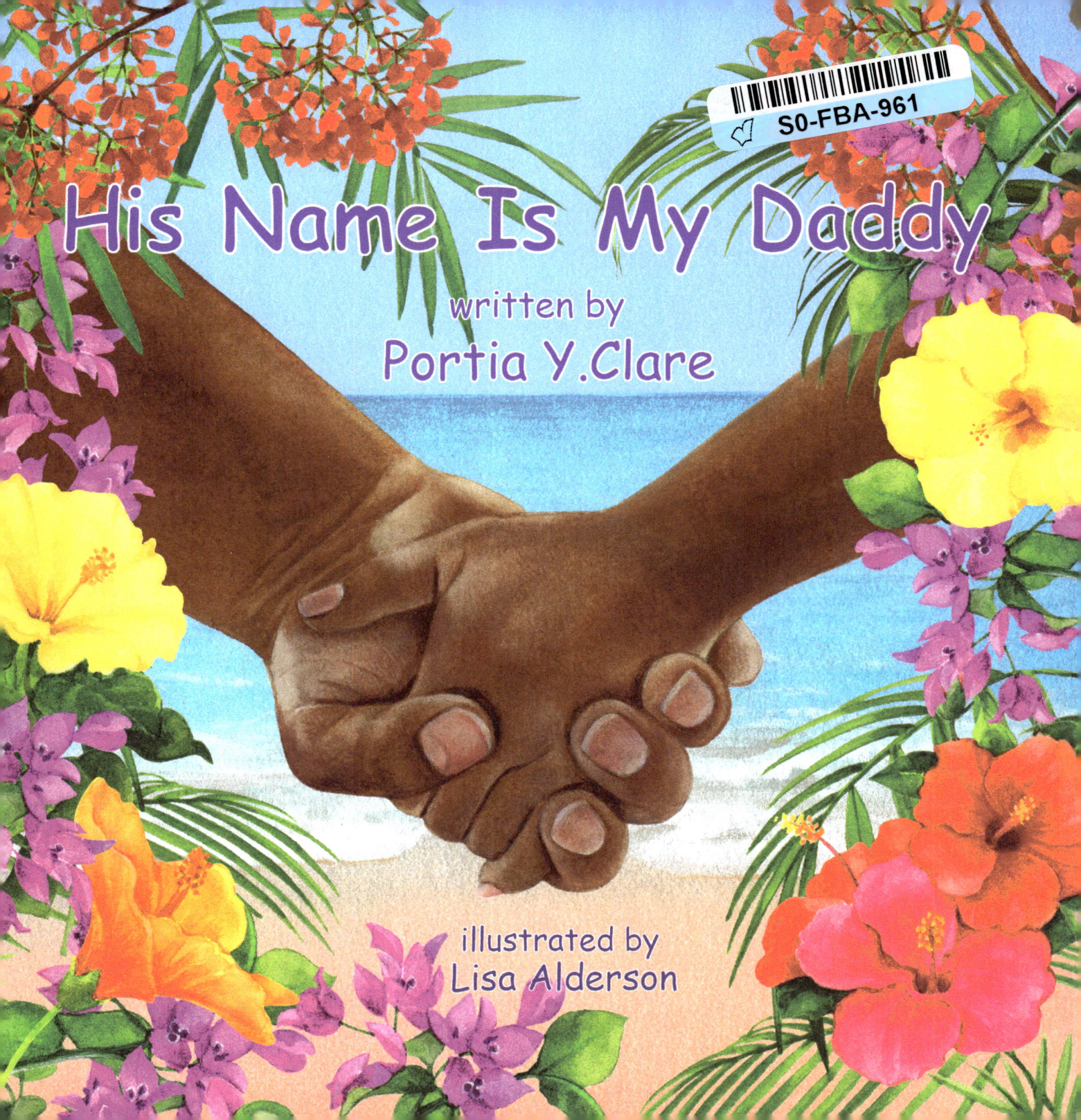

Xulon Press
2301 Lucien Way #415
Maitland, FL 32751
407.339.4217
www.xulonpress.com

© 2023 by Portia Y. Clare

Illustrated by Lisa Alderson

All rights reserved solely by the author. The author guarantees all contents are original and do not infringe upon
the legal rights of any other person or work. No part of this book may be reproduced in any form without the permission of the author.

Due to the changing nature of the Internet, if there are any web addresses, links, or URLs included in this manuscript, these may have been altered and may no longer be accessible. The views and opinions shared in this book belong solely to the author and do not necessarily reflect those of the publisher. The publisher therefore disclaims responsibility for the views or opinions expressed within the work.

Unless otherwise indicated, Scripture quotations taken from the
King James Version (KJV)–*public domain.*

Paperback ISBN-13: 978-1-66287-004-0
Hard Cover ISBN-13: 978-1-66287-005-7
Ebook ISBN-13: 978-1-66287-006-4

To
My Daddy
and
My Mommy,
From My Heart to Yours

"Scoop, did you just call home? The phone rang once and stopped ringing when my hand touched it. You know, our phone has been acting up, and I thought you might have been trying to reach me," he said.

As I stood listening to his voice, I envisioned his hand holding the telephone receiver. I will always remember his hands — those enormous, well-seasoned, appendages. Just one of them concealed my entire face!

Proportional to his six-foot, two-and-a-half inch, 270-pound frame, those massive hands were always a part of my life. They belonged to a loving and caring man who many referred to as Randy. But I still call him "My Daddy."

I remember My Daddy's hands when he taught me how to bowl left-handed when I was nine years old.

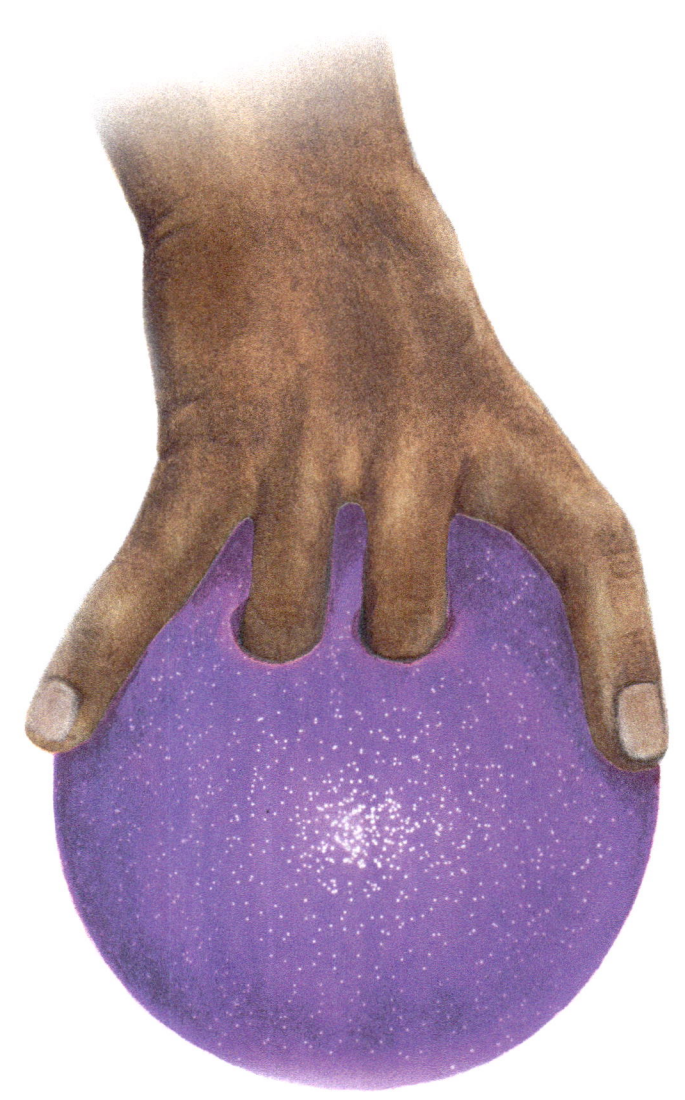

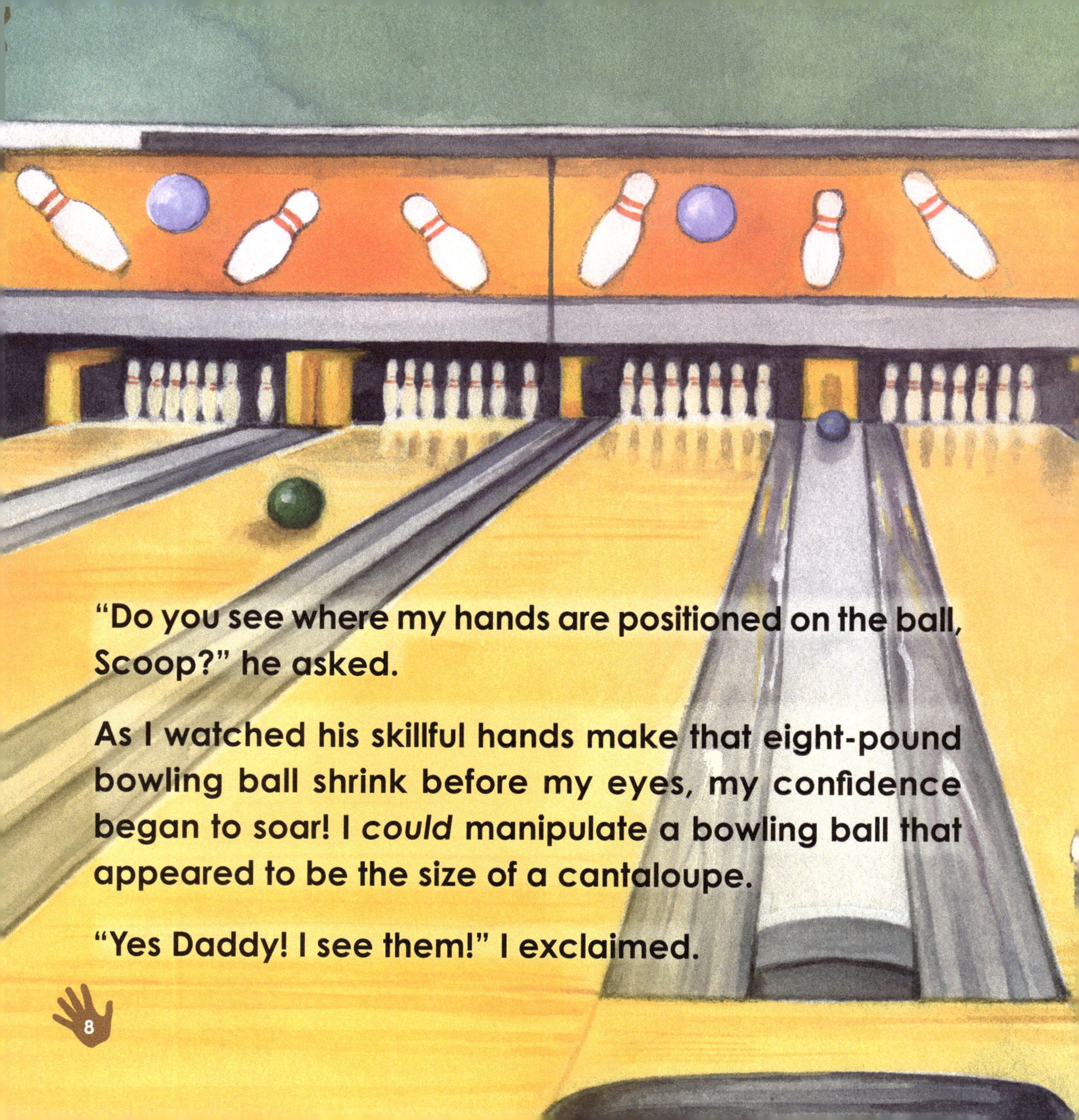

"Do you see where my hands are positioned on the ball, Scoop?" he asked.

As I watched his skillful hands make that eight-pound bowling ball shrink before my eyes, my confidence began to soar! I *could* manipulate a bowling ball that appeared to be the size of a cantaloupe.

"Yes Daddy! I see them!" I exclaimed.

Then, placing the bowling ball in my hands, he molded his hands with mine and transformed me into a left-handed bowler in one Saturday afternoon.

I became "Bowler of the Year" the following season.

I remember My Daddy's hands when he sowed and sacrificed for me.

"Don't worry about the cost of your tuition, Scooplex. It will get paid. The Lord will provide. You just concentrate on your studies. Remember, nothing is too good for 'My Daughter the Car'!" he assured.

My Daddy called me "My Daughter the Car" because my first name, Portia, sounded just like the name of the car, Porsche!

Reaching a resourceful hand into his pocket, he asked, "Now, do you need any money for anything?"

"But, Daddy, you can't afford…"

"Trust me, Scoop. Here, take this. And no 'buts'!" he insisted.

Gently placing the folded bills in my palm, he enclosed my hand in his and gave it a reassuring squeeze.

My tuition was paid in full at commencement.

I remember My Daddy's hands when he introduced me to Joshua 1:8 and 9.

As his hands held the Scriptures, he quickly found the exact book, chapter, and verse, showing how familiar he was with the text.

"Pointing to the verses, he proclaimed, "Ah, here we go, Scoop! Listen to this. 'This book of the law shall not depart out of thy mouth; but thou shalt meditate therein day and night, that thou mayest observe to do according to all that is written therein: for then thou shalt make thy way prosperous, and then thou shalt have good success. Have not I commanded thee? Be strong and of a good courage; be not afraid, neither be thou dismayed: for the Lord thy God is with thee whithersoever thou goest.'"

As he read the verses from my Bible, my eyes followed his fingers.

With unshakable confidence and my Sword now an extension of My Daddy's hand, he declared, "You trust in the Lord, Scooplex. I am telling you. I am persuaded that you will never be confounded or confused. I have never seen the righteous forsaken or his seed made to beg bread. Search the Scriptures, Scooplex. In them, you will find life and peace."

Joshua 1:8 and 9 are my favorite Bible verses.

I remember My Daddy's hands when he disciplined me.

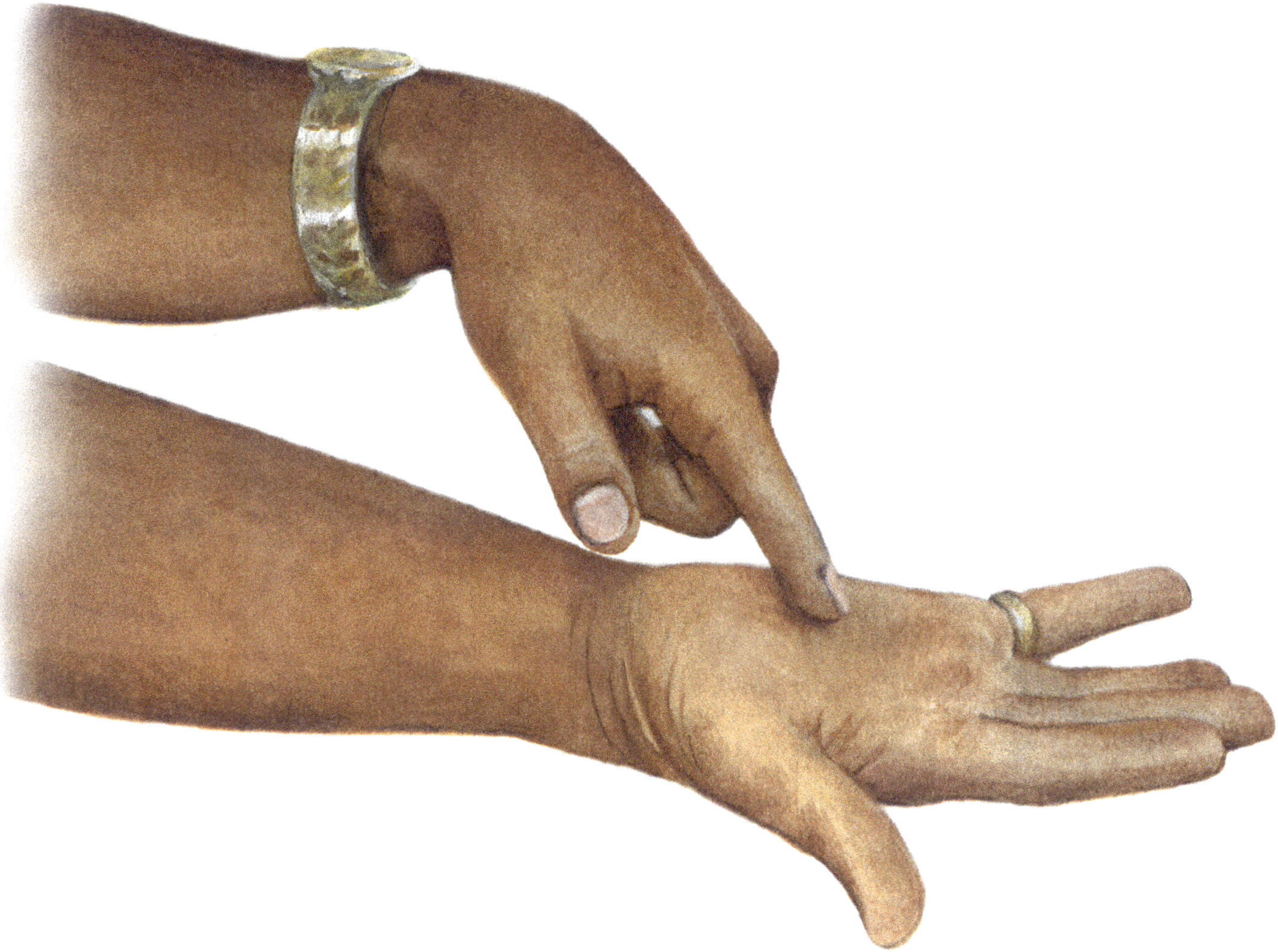

His hands were never used to correct me harshly. His very presence commanded my respect and obedience. The sound of his hands applauding reminded me of thunder. His grip was powerful and as secure as a promise he made to me.

Yet, his embrace was endearing and as soft and comforting as a goose down pillow on a rainy day.

My Daddy's hands exemplified power under control.

As My Daddy's hands grew older, they often ached and swelled with arthritis.

But they still reflected his strength and character and represented that which was an essential part of my life.

My hands, which strongly resemble My Daddy's hands, are an extension of him. They are a constant reminder of his never-ending unconditional love, support, encouragement, and commitment, to the end, to me.

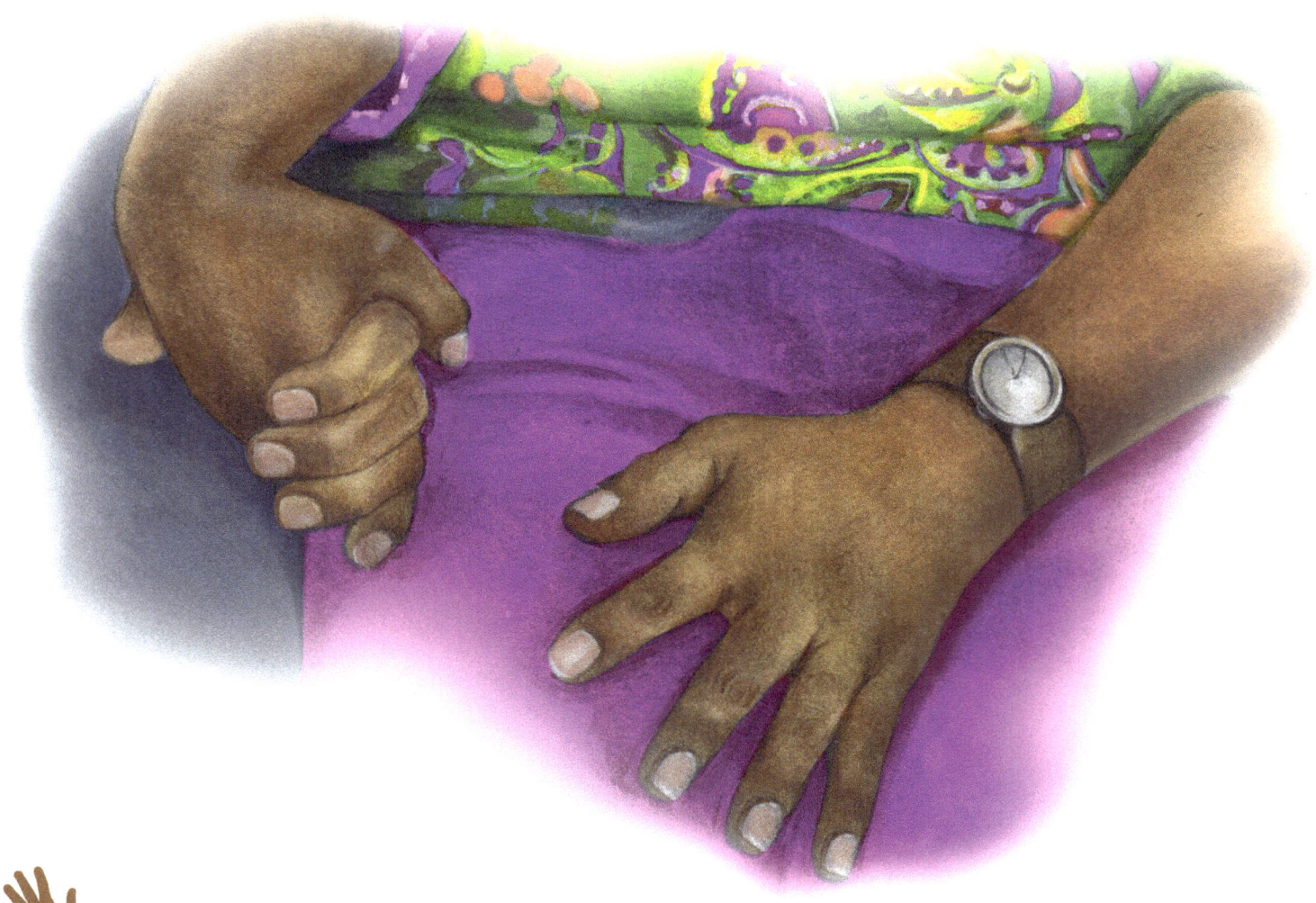

My Daddy's hand was resting in mine when he went home to be with Jesus.

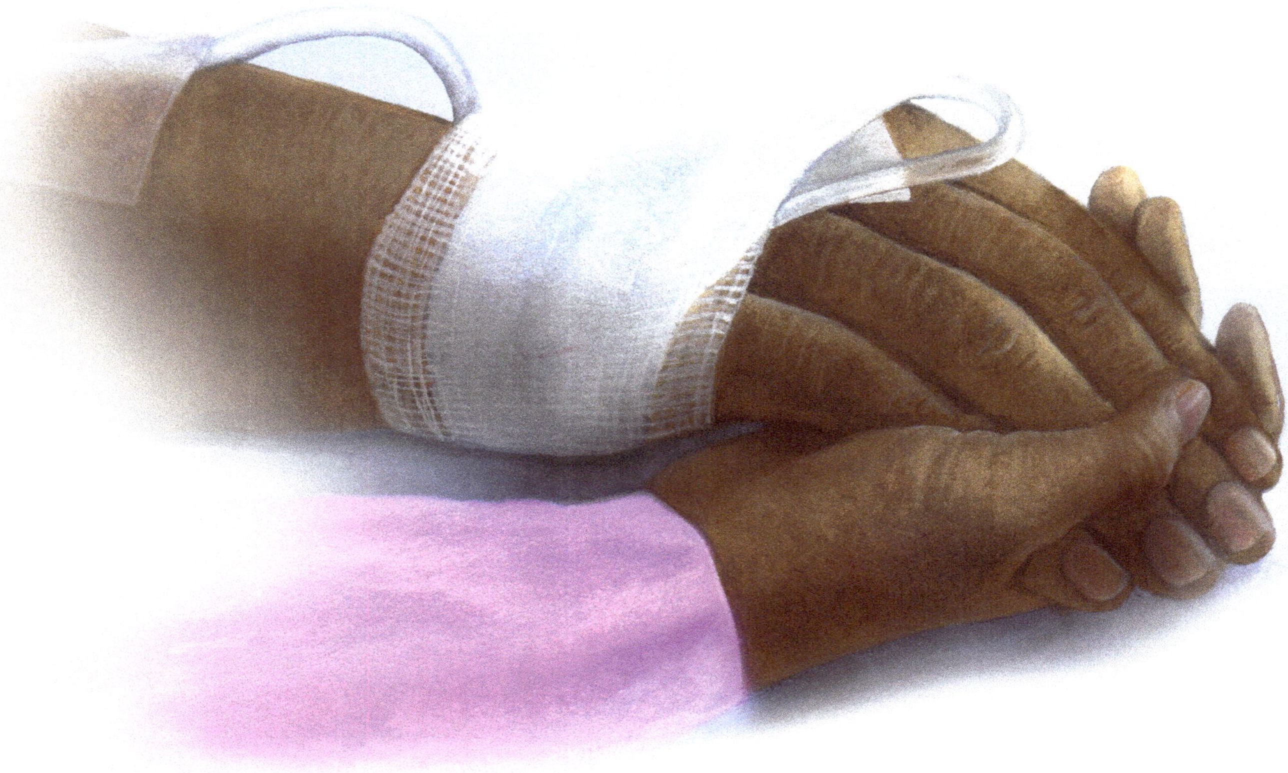

I LOVE YOU FOREVER, My Daddy! Thank you for everything! I cannot wait to hold your hand again someday!

A Reflection for Parents and Children

My Daddy is the basis for this book. He was a light and an anchor for me, his child; our Heavenly Father is a light and an anchor for us, His children. My relationship with My Daddy here on earth was my first example of building trust and faith in a father. My Daddy was my first example of seeing a father who loved unconditionally and who was faithful to his word. He taught me when I rose in the morning, when I walked by the way, and when I lay down at night. My Daddy taught me how to trust and have a relationship with our Heavenly Father through his example to me as an earthly father. My Daddy made it easier for me to love and follow a God who I could not see by allowing me to see God's character through his words and his actions. My Daddy built a bridge that allowed me to reach, accept, and establish a personal and life-changing relationship, through Jesus Christ, with a loving, omnipotent, omniscient, and omnipresent Heavenly Father.

May this book serve to help and encourage you to build and cross that same bridge.

God bless you.

About the Author

Portia Yvette Clare has been privileged to serve in developing the minds and character of children for over thirty years. She believes that she was born to teach. Her love of children compels her to write stories that help them to recognize their quality, appreciate their value, and navigate through difficult life experiences. *His Name is My Daddy*, her second children's book, is a true story. She is also the author of the best-selling, award winning children's book, *Best Friends Forever: A Puppy's Tale*.

Portia is the only child of the late Randolph George Clare, Jr. and Jane Easterling Clare. She and her mother currently reside in Bennettsville, South Carolina.

For more information about her books, school visits, presentations, and activities, please visit Portia's website at portiayclare.com.

About the Illustrator

Lisa Alderson was born in the UK and grew up with a love of drawing and nature. She followed this passion with a degree in Scientific and Natural History Illustration. This has led to a diverse career working as a freelance illustrator for many clients internationally. She currently lives in a small village near York, UK, with her husband, twins, and Hobbes, the dog.